Download the accompanying yoga story at
www.childrensyoga.com/fffyogastory.php

$2 per sale of this book are donated to
Shanti Bhavan
www.shantibhavanonline.org

**To my father, Howard (Howdy) Meyers, who loved to enjoy life.
May his soul ever be blessed.**
—Shakta Kaur Khalsa

**To Guru Fateh Singh, my son, who knows
how to obey, serve, love, excel.**
—Siri-Kartar K. Khalsa

Text copyright © 2000 by Shakta Kaur Khalsa

Book and cover design: schererMedia

Illustrations by Siri-Kartar K. Khalsa

Manufactured in Mexico

Khalsa, Shakta Kaur, 1950-
   The five-fingered family / [retold] by Shakta
Kaur Khalsa ; illustrated by Siri-Kartar K.
Khalsa. -- 1st ed.
    p. cm.
    LCCN: 99-76581
    ISBN: 0-9660172-9-3
    SUMMARY: A retelling of the ancient Punjabi
tale in which a family survives the loss of their
weaving workshop, and wrests a treasure from a
troll because of the way they stick together.

   1. Tales--India--Punjab. 2. Punjabis (South
Asian people)--Folklore. I. Khalsa, Siri-Kartar
K. II. Title

PZ8.1.K43Fi 2000   398.23/2545
[E]   QBI99-1880

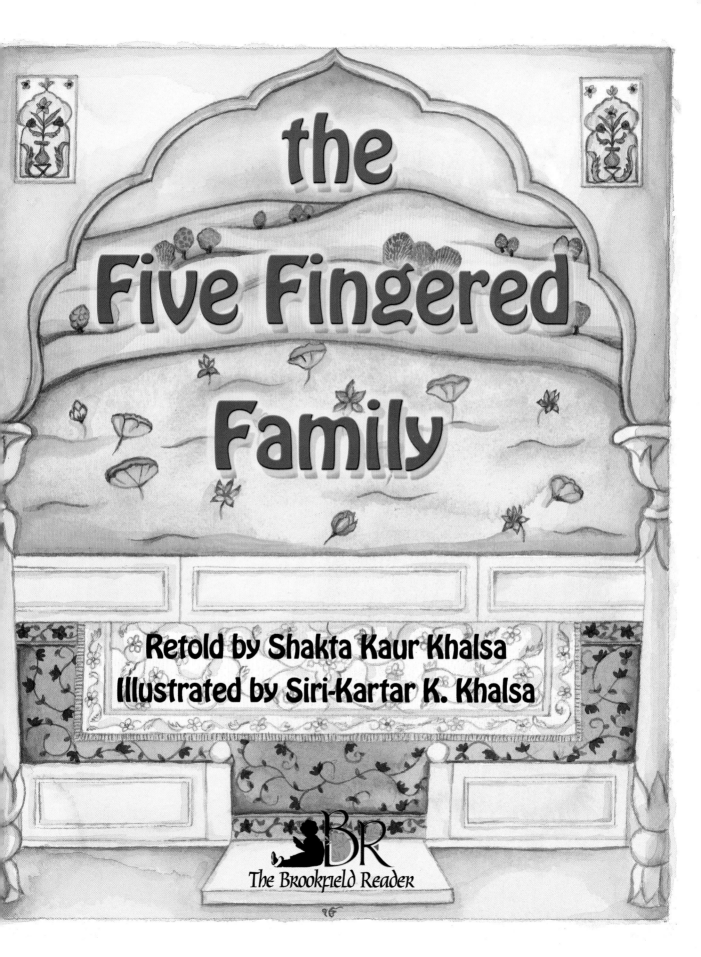

the
Five Fingered
Family

Retold by Shakta Kaur Khalsa
Illustrated by Siri-Kartar K. Khalsa

The Brookfield Reader

n the magical land of India, there once lived a family with a story to tell. They were Papa Angulee, Mama Angulee and their three children. In their native language of Punjabi, the word "angulee" means finger. Each day their quick fingers spun and wove sheep's wool into cloth. This was their family business.

ow everything went along just fine, until one day they arrived to work only to find that a fire had destroyed their workshop and everything in it. Papa Angulee sat his family down on some rocks beside the smoldering remains of their building and quietly spoke, "There is no other work in this town that we can do. I know of another town nearby where we can find the work we need."

For a moment everyone was quiet. Then Mama Angulee got up from her stony seat and in her bravest voice said, "All right, children. Let's go home and pack now!" And everyone did.

n their way to the next town, they had to pass through a dark forest. As night was falling, they came to a very large pipal tree with thick, spreading branches. Papa Angulee stopped. "We will eat here and spend the night under this pipal tree. It will provide shelter for us in case of rain." He began clearing the ground of sticks to make a soft place to sleep.

Meanwhile, Mama Angulee gave jobs to the children, saying, "My sons, go to the river and bring back buckets of water for cooking. Daughter, you and I will gather wood for the fire. Then we will all help prepare the food."

Each set out to do their chores. Though the buckets were heavy, the sons did their best to lug them up from the river. The daughter gathered small twigs to start the fire and dragged large branches to keep it going. Everyone chopped the vegetables. Soon there was a bright fire with a big pot of soup cooking.

he aroma of that soup floated up, up, up into the big pipal tree. It drifted into a dark, leafy corner where there lived a forest spirit—a dark spirit that is sometimes called a troll.

The troll had been watching this family the whole time with great interest since it was also his dinnertime. When he saw how unified this family was, he was surprised. But he said to himself, "I am so great, I can easily make them mine!" So he jumped down from the tree, hoping to scare the father who was chopping more wood.

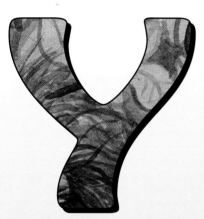ou have nothing to cook, so why are you making a fire?" the troll snarled.

Papa Angulee made no sign of surprise or fear at the ugly-looking creature crouching in front of him. He looked the troll straight in the eyes and calmly said, "We are going to cook and eat you!"

his surprised the troll even more. He looked at the rest of the family who had stopped working and were eyeing him with the same fearless look. He began to be a bit afraid of these people. He thought, "This family has five people, and they are like a hand with five fingers. You cannot take them apart and use them against each other. They know how to work together. If I know what's good for me, I'd better be nice to them!"

So the troll pleaded with the father, "Please don't eat me. Dig a big hole under this tree, and you will find a great treasure there. You can have it— just leave me alone!"

he five-fingered family worked together to dig up the ground, and sure enough, there was the treasure—gold, silver, jewels— more than they had ever seen in their lives!

They took it home, bought another business and returned to a happy life.

ow, right next door to the Angulee family lived another family called the Lobhas. Mr. Lobha noticed that the Angulees had plenty of money, so he went to pay them a visit. As he sat with Papa Angulee, his desire for wealth made him impatient, and he blurted out, "You were poor, but now you have lots of money. How did that happen?"

As Papa Angulee told the story, Mr. Lobha's head was swimming with thoughts of the big tree, the troll and, most especially, the treasure box. He could already see himself fingering gold coins and rubies. His heart burning with greed, he rushed home to his wife, saying, "Let's try our luck with this troll!"

So they went out into the deep forest, found the pipal tree and set out to do the same things that the other family had done. But when Mr. Lobha told his son to go out and gather wood, the son complained, "But it rained last night. I can't find any dry wood. You find it!"

And when Mrs. Lobha asked the other children to get water from the river for cooking, they whined, "But it's too far, and the water will be too heavy. You'd better do it!"

t this, the father and mother got angry and began to yell at their children. The children, in turn, began bickering among themselves, saying, "You should get the water. You are older!" And, "Don't boss me around. I don't have to listen to you!"

Then Mr. Lobha turned to his wife, yelling, "This is all your fault! Why don't you make them obey?"

To which she retorted, "Oh, so they are my children. You have nothing to do with it?"

he troll was, of course, listening to all this from his high perch in the dark, leafy part of the tree. With a nasty laugh he dropped down from the tree and stood facing the family. "What are you going to cook?" asked the troll slyly.

Remembering what Papa Angulee told him, Mr. Lobha said, "We are going to cook you!"

hen the troll made himself large and monstrous, and he said, "You are trying to be like the first family, but it will not work. They were united, like fingers of a hand. And so they were very strong against me. But you, on the other hand, do not know how to obey. Each of you cares only about yourself. You cannot eat me. Instead you will be my dinner!"

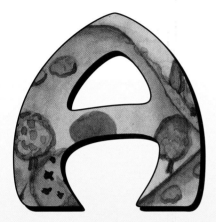nd so saying, he reached out to grab them. Just at that moment, this divided family united in one thought. They grabbed hands, and while holding tightly onto one another, ran as fast as they could back to their town. Sweating, tired and without treasure, they arrived home safely.

The troll, realizing he was defeated, crept back into the dark forest. "Next time somebody comes along I won't waste time talking. I'll just take them by surprise!" he grumbled to himself as he took his perch in the pipal tree.

ow did it go?" asked Papa Angulee the next day when he saw Mr. Lobha outside in his yard. Mr. Lobha explained all that had happened and how they had helped each other escape. "We are so happy to be alive!" he exclaimed.

When he saw the change in his neighbor, Papa Angulee's face broke into a wide smile, and he said, "So it sounds like you got your treasure after all!"

Then they both had a good laugh.

AUTHOR'S NOTES

THE FIVE FINGERED FAMILY has been told, with many variations, in the Punjab region of Northern India for many years. The story came to me by way of Bibiji Inderjit Kaur, whose grandmother told stories to her when she was a little girl. Bibiji would sit on Grandma's bed, along with her siblings and cousins, and Grandma would relay story after story—of heroes and heroines, good and evil and real and imaginary creatures. What they all had in common was the thread of integrity: the theme of spirit winning over darkness.

Bibiji wrote a book called STORIES TO WIN THE WORLD, and in that book I found this story. I have adapted it to speak to young children as well as older ones. In my retelling, the families have names that are significant. For example, Angulee in punjabi means "finger" and Lobha means "greed." The pipal tree that is central to the story also has meaning. The pipal tree, with its heart-shaped leaves is held in reverence in India. It is said that Lord Krishna was born under a pipal tree.

The illustrations, done by my friend and spiritual sister, Siri-Kartar K. Khalsa, warmly color the soft and vibrant mood of India. The style used for the settings and costumes are typical of the people of the Punjab, and most specifically, those of the Sikh faith. Siri-Kartar and I both have a great affinity for the Punjab, and we bring that love to the text and the illustrations.